DID I WAKE YOU?

BETH LAPIDES

Soft Skull Press
Brooklyn, New York
2006

Did I Wake You?
© 2007 by Beth Lapides

ISBN-13: 978-1-933368-49-8
ISBN-10: 1-933368-49-7

Published by Soft Skull Press
55 Washington St, Suite 804
Brooklyn NY 11201
www.softskull.com

Distributed by Publishers Group West
www.pgw.com 1-800-788-3123

Book design by Peter Karras

Library of Congress Cataloging-in-Publication Data
Lapides, Beth.
  Did I wake you? / Beth Lapides.
     p. cm.
  I I. Title.
PS3612.A643D53 2006
811'.6--dc22
2006026916

Printed In Canada

"When asked whether he was a god or a man, Buddha replied simply, 'I am awake'"

—LAMA SURYA DAS

"Wake me up before you go-go
Cause I'm not planning on going solo"

—WHAM!

For everyone who's woken me up—
Most especially Greg Miller, who wakes me
up to love every minute of every day—and
Teddy who taught me that the real trick to
waking up is being able to fall asleep.

INTRODUCTION

I finally had an office of my own. Not a corner of the kitchen. Not a chair in the bedroom. Not half of Greg's office. An actual office of my own. With room for my desk, my art, my keyboard. Even all my inspirational paraphernalia/junk. And I was petrified.

I was afraid of not having the excuse of not having an office any more. Afraid of the extremes I'd gone to in order to get the office. Afraid I'd be lonely. Afraid it would be too cold in the winter and too hot in the summer. I was afraid of the cartons I still had to unpack. Who needs monsters when you have your life packed up in boxes, waiting to confront you with each slice of the X-acto knife. Which reminded me of all the things not in this office that I was afraid of, too. Airports, lying governments, that it was too late.

"Don't be afraid," I told myself. But it wasn't working. It never works when you tell yourself not to do something. Your brain only hears the *something*, not the *don't*. "Don't eat" sounds like "Eat!" That's why sometimes, when you go on a diet, you gain weight. At least, that's what I tell myself.

So, you can't even tell yourself not to tell yourself not to do things. You have to think of the thing that you do need to do in order to not have room in the time/space continuum of your life for the thing that you don't want to do anymore. Like tell yourself to be OK with being a little hungry. That way you won't eat. Or tell yourself to focus on love. That way you won't have room for the fear.

And I was trying to focus on love. How much I loved my house, this office, Greg who'd helped me get it, the mountain I could see out the window. I focused on loving myself and giving myself a break for being afraid, since the fact is that moving is the second most stressful thing in life. The first being someone you love dying. It occurred to me that the stress is so high when you move because, in a sense, when you move, you die. Of course, in the best-case scenario, you're reborn also. But I hadn't been reborn yet and was anxious. Which is just another way of saying afraid. Plus my hands were really dirty. The thing about moving is you have to touch everything you own, especially the old dusty stuff, because only by touching something can you determine if the thing is just a thing or if it's a portal to another dimension.

One carton scared me the most. It was the carton filled with my stand-up comedy notes from the past ten years. But I felt that I had to read these notes before I filed them away, since more than I was dreading reliving the past ten years, I had a sense that I had wasted that time because nothing had come from this work.

Of course something had come from that work. Lots of things. All the things on my resume from the past ten years had, in a sense, come from that work. Nevertheless I was haunted by a feeling that I'd wasted all that time and wanted something to come from that work more directly. Even though I knew all those nights on stage had been something. Something big. But like all performance, documented though it may be, the *something* that it is is something ephemeral. And I had a longing for something concrete. A book of essays seemed the most likely. Maybe a script. In my wildest dreams the TV show that would finally go. Maybe a novel. Something.

The pile of paper was over a foot high. I replaced my fear with love. My love of strong coffee, a mug of which I gripped as I strapped on my love of the hunt. And I began reading. I was circling things with my red pen, tossing pages, staying open. Then I started seeing the haikus.

The first ones were some I'd written to perform—as haikus. They'd been welcome solid rocks in the stream of consciousness that is my stand-up. And then I started seeing that dozens of chunks I'd written in shorthand for performance were actually fully formed haikus. And there were hundreds more that were very close. Maybe I had to flip a line, or add a syllable, but for the most part there, in my mountain of paper, in the course of a week, I found over five hundred haikus!

Good morning! OK, I did edit many out and write some more for the book as it exists now. But basically, there it was. Splashing cold water on my face. Waking me up to waking up. What's the point of wanting there to be a book of essays where a book of haikus already exists?

And then I started looking at my life differently. What answers was I overlooking while I was busy trying to see the answers that I wished were there? So many! And so, against all odds, I am publishing a book of haikus.

My dream is that every time you see the *Did I Wake You?* spine on your bookshelf, you're reminded that what you're looking for may not be what you're looking for. That you open up to answers you may not have preconceived. And aren't afraid that the answers aren't there. And you love the process. And, maybe later, the TV show will come.

♥∞—Beth
Palm Springs (that's another story)
2006 (or so they say)

DIRTY OPTIMISM

It's like the best of
times and the worst of times but
without the best of.

"Did I wake you?" "No."
"Are you sure?" "Well, kind of." "I'll
call back." "I'm up now!"

Magical thinking's
not thinking—or magic. But it's
better than panic.

Finished a draft of
"Best Case Scenario" on
9/10. Scratch that.

"I love," Tim said, "that
you're thinking 'throw a party.'
I'm thinking, 'xanax.'"

"You're so negative
for a positive person,"
he said. "No I'm not!"

A born optimist,
I fell away. Got depressed.
Came crawling back home.

Afternoon is tough.
The hope of morning's spent, dark
courage not yet here.

I stopped to smell the
roses. But the roses did
not smell. Tried again.

Slavery? Hitler?
The plague? The Ice Age? When
were those good old days?

The glass isn't half
full. It is full. Half tainted
water. Half bad air.

"Being number two
is very under-rated,"
said sad number three.

There's no us and them.
But still, we're not them. Are we?
Are we even us?

Melting pot sounds: hum
buzz, coo and cluck. Umlauted
vowels, bring good luck.

Every snowflake's
unique 'til it merges with
the blanket. Then, slush.

No astrology
in GQ. Well dressed men think:
fate's in my own hands.

Fear keeps me awake.
Gratitude puts me to sleep.
Love says good morning.

HOLLYWOOD MATH

When I said be more
Liz Taylor—I meant diamonds,
not back pain and pills.

The absence of yes,
over time, is equal to
no. Hollywood Math.

It's not what you know
or who you know—it's who knows
you and what they know.

Ben Affleck and I
reach for the last coconut
shrimp. And I get it!

Hollywood asks: How
big's your name? Kabbalah asks:
eat bread of shame? Same.

"Salma Hayek went
behind my desk and ate all
my Pirate Booty."

She was an artist,
then an entertainer, then
finally, product.

"If I don't get a
job soon I might be forced to
take an acting class."

Oscar Mania
slows traffic, puts egos on
fast track. Distracts me.

Good Thai dinner is
ruined by table of Kevin
Bacon film-namers.

One billion is a
thousand millions. Bill Gates has
ninety-nine of those.

Larry King asks Tom
Cruise, "Any regrets?" "No, no!
Larry, I'm Tom Cruise!"

Charlie Rose dresses
down for Sean Penn, who dresses
up for Charlie Rose.

Holy Hollywood—
where God is in the details
of your deal memo.

Jacqueline Suzanne.
Mae West. Katherine Hepburn.
Three ladies I like.

ARE YOU BORED WITH YOUR TEETH?

Ad asked, "Are you bored
with your teeth?" Not ashamed, bored.
Go America!

"Mayan calendar's
end, predicts shift," radio
says. I shift. Park. Shop.

Returned the gas mask.
Didn't know where to keep it.
Home? Car? LeSport Sac?

"My uncle bought a
life size bronze gorilla—I
was in the bathroom."

One hundred percent
acrylic. Fine. But leave off
the picture of sheep.

Nothing sours a
sweet bargain more quickly than
a parking ticket.

10k a pop for
fertility treatments. Use
Visa, get the miles.

"Suit I bought? At
Saks? That made my skin itch? Snake
eggs in the lining."

"My wife's an artist,"
says my car salesman. "She
paints. Mostly Van Goghs."

"Decorate, but don't
spend too much, you'll move again
soon—or you'll die."

"I like my car so
much I want to go outside
and fuck it right now."

Good shopping today.
Bought a fancy-ass bag
to get a life for.

Smelled every perfume
in Sephora—looking good's
good—smelling's more-a.

A sign that we have too
much stuff: it's falling on our
heads and killing us.

"You don't have money for a flag but you do for water," he accused.

DEAR DIARY,

Trying to replace
my feelings of vague dread with
specific concerns.

Eradicating
fear fails. Substituting love
for fear is lovely.

So tired, I drank
some "get up and go" so I
could lay down and rest.

I surrender to
God. But I am God so I
surrender to me.

I try not to judge
people for not struggling.
More struggle for me.

Went the whole summer
without one Frappuccino.
A small victory.

Ways that I have changed:
I don't cry when I pack and
I can stand on my head.

We're one now. But two
still too. One and two. Not not
one and not not two.

Standing at the sink.
Spoon after spoon of soy nut
butter. So easy.

I don't want to live
in my past, but I do want
someone to live there.

If I include them
but they don't include me
that makes me bigger.

Oy to the vey! My
parents came to visit but
bought a house instead.

People say, "You'll see...
you'll have kids someday." Maybe
they'll see. Since I'm me.

Book idea: "Soy
Doesn't Foam, and Other Lies
Baristas Told Me."

"It's only a phase,"
she said. And okay, sure, but
isn't everything?

Fantasizing that
I was too busy to have
the feelings that I do.

A broken egg at
the foot of the stairs of my
apartment. Bad sign.

My friend did something
I'm against. Even so, I'm
for her doing it.

Broke up with my plan,
and city and hair. After
my landlord dumped me.

Lawn sprinklers spritz.
Small rainbows hover. And I'm
somewhere over them.

A NUN @
THE GYNECOLOGIST'S

Lolita poster
in Agnes B. Kids. Are they
asleep or kidding?

I'm an expert at
being a beginner. So,
beginner or not?

She asked, "Will you speak
about the healing power
of laughter?" "Yes," I sobbed.

"Why've you got a
giant octopus tattoo?"
"Oh, no real reason."

Never read Proust—feel
I have—have read Sartre but
feel that I haven't.

I am curious
what would it feel like to be
not so curious.

Restrictions become
freeing, comfort foods become
uncomfortable.

Jewish at Christmas.
I'm a tourist—knowing words
but the accent's wrong.

When I miss you I
watch the weather channel. What's
it like where you are?

He's got a diamond
stud in his ear and asks if
Cobb salad's too femme.

Bad for my skin to
sit in the sun but good to
be kissed by a star.

"That seat is saved. It's
my friend's." But it is not. Saved
or his. Just a seat.

Analyzing my
want, I found it was wanting
want, not wanting me.

I'm against herd think
'til I start my myspace page
then I'm all "herd here."

He thought in numbers.
She thought in words. They divorced
in sign language.

You can't live with them,
you can't get born without them:
mommies, mothers, moms.

Don't think of "pain." Think
of "sensation." OK, yeah,
painful sensation.

The fake fireplace
demanded attention—then
delivered nothing.

Boss called me in, said:
"It's not over yet." Which meant:
"It is over now."

"You don't have to tell
us everything—from now on—
nothing about sperm."

Blind man's entering
the Getty. To smell the oils?
Listen to watching?

Starting to suspect
that letting the day unfold
is seizing the day.

DUST BUNNIES

"Wrote the number of
my ex by my phone then—'for
pain—call this number'"

If you're going to
kill ants, is it better to
enjoy it or not?

Fear's like a toddler.
I just can't bear to say no
every single time.

CD player is
set on random play but keeps
playing the same track.

The world is so clean
that injecting asthmatics
with dirt helps them breathe.

"He won't let it go."
"He deals antiques, not letting
things go is his job."

Woke up worried I
won't know first aid if there's war.
Changed bedtime reading.

Dad, friends, big brother.
Aliens, terrorists, God.
You are not alone.

Turns out, obsession
with health is unhealthy—but
better than Splenda.

Is it possible
to have bad chemistry with
an entire country?

The reason for war—
as well as for bored: lack of
imagination.

This yoga teacher's
annoying. Talks and talks and
reminds me of me.

The dark smell of toast.
Reassuring, alluring.
Danger to my thighs.

No no I'm not no
I'm not in denial no
no no no no no.

MY FIREWALL
NEEDS WORK

Mauve jacaranda
blooms fall onto the headline:
TERROR THIS SUMMER!

No dust storms today.
The Rover's solar groovy.
Or so NASA says.

Cinquo de Mayo,
A total mess in Iraq.
Oh me oh my oh.

China's got toxic
dust storms—expanding deserts—
and they just got E!

I hate when a war
is the first time I've ever even
heard of a country.

Fear of dancing to
the fear drum of news trumps my
fear of not knowing.

Arnold says, "Failure's
not an option." Which is a
failure on his part.

Anticipating
future crises keeps me from
noticing this one.

P.S. They found a
new galaxy and a new
form of matter too.

Ruggy's a Muppet
they made to teach kids not to
step on the land mines.

We're "target rich." Parks.
Farms. Harbors. Reservoirs. Plus
all of those Targets.

Upside to bird flu:
spy satellites track the birds,
less time to track me.

Borders are too tight.
Belts are too tight. Breathing is
hard. Lips are too loose.

Watching the world change
changes the world but not so
much you can see it.

Facts are like one night
stands—hard to remember and
they never add up.

They're trying to clone
Jesus. Wouldn't he say we're
all Christ already?

I do handstands—Life
in this Empire makes me want
to know how to fall.

Emotional facts.
Retro new wave. Transluscent
Concrete. This is now.

Panic fills me when
he says, "certainly you've heard
of..." and I have not.

Unsubscribing to
all three of my newspapers
caused giddy free fall.

SO MANY CLOCKS,
SO LITTLE TIME

Slow cars make Greg ask:
"Don't they want to get where they're
going?" No, they don't.

Tantric sex is hot.
Unfortunately it's also
quite time consuming.

"Mario Cuomo
gets so much done." Of course,
he runs no errands.

Need to get a test,
which means driving and waiting,
peeing and paying.

The modern mouth's got
a superhero sheen—it's
applied on the move.

If you clone yourself
you still won't get enough sleep
or vacation more.

Poles shifting. And what
was twenty-four hours is
now sixteen. Not sweet.

Beauty cracks the whip.
Demanding. A total top.
A reason to stop.

Continue to hold
for the next available operator:
practicing patience.

Five hundred billion
galaxies. Never even
been to Italy.

I'm tired of facts.
They make me sleepy and dull
and keep me from sex.

ET's will come in
the summer—they won't want to
compete with Christmas.

Stars dot the skies. Dots
dot your i's. Infinity's
dot dot dot. Not com.

It's not the alarm's
fault I need waking. Not my
fault I need deep sleep.

STOP TOUCHING YOUR FACE

While waiting for the
other shoe to drop, put the
first shoe back on.

Why do today what
you can put off forever?
Take a nap instead.

Getting enough sleep
means letting go sooner. Or
giving enough sleep.

If you drive yourself
crazy then you're taking jobs
from other people.

When in Rome, do as
much as possible and think:
I am in Rome now!

The early bird gets
the worm but the night owl gets
the starry eyed sky.

Just cause it's raining
it doesn't mean you have to
wear ill-fitting pants.

Stopped searching Google.
Started searching my soul. It
said get back online.

Worry's the devil.
Don't worry about it though
or the devil wins.

Don't go to bed mad.
No nervous breakdowns after
midnight. Two good rules.

Strong features—smudgy
make-up. Weak features—strong lines.
Wish I'd known sooner.

Come from love or fear.
Only two choices really.
And sometimes no choice.

Everything I know
I learned at Home Depot or
possibly at Lowes.

A time to sow and
a time to reap. Reaping's a
better show. So sow.

Sleeping on it is
an actual tactic, and
a pleasure to boot.

Truth's got lies licked. Art's
got shlock blocked. But beauty's got
ugly up its ass.

Front is the ego.
Back is the universal.
Middle's the new edge.

Check for the pieces.
Self assembly required.
IKEA and life.

Blue girl cries under
insanely blue skies. Blue balled
guy wondering why.

Everything's perfect?
Even my doubt about it
all being perfect?

"Would you like a twist?"
"Yes," I always say, feeling
the truth of the phrase.

Tech support. Household
help. Roadside assistance. Life—
don't try it alone.

"Buck it up! Take the
pain! Feel the burn. Pussy! Wimp!"
Real encouragement?

Starting a family?
More people should think about
ending a family.

Exfoliating
won't lead to world peace but does
remove old dead stuff.

Curiosity
killed the cat but it also
mapped our DNA.

TYPE A FREE SPIRIT

Went on Weight Watchers.
Didn't lose any weight but
enjoyed the boundaries.

It's a gift to be
simple. A gift I wasn't
given. Lucky me.

I am a girl who has
waited. But usually,
not waited alone.

I like those pants but
they are far too noisy for
the world we live in.

My computer laughs
at me every fifteen minutes.
Cause I set it that way.

I drink while I write.
I've smoked pot too—so sue me.
Crazy Haiku Chick.

I know it's a good
idea if I feel thin while
I am thinking it.

I like my showers
the way I like my men—with
adjustable heads.

My ship's come in but
it needs unloading and the
workers are on strike.

You broke my heart and
taught me how to stay and I
practiced it today.

The first time I came
to LA I almost died.
Best part of the trip.

I dated a guy
who was all man. He crushed me.
Blamed me. Walked too fast.

The foam's so soft. The
world's so not. My beverage
and I—both so hot.

Velcro, gather, join.
Link, center, merge.
Thank you thesaurus.

I put on lip goo
in the car and in the loo.
Before I see you.

I am the hum. The
hum is my home. When the hum
is gone, I am alone.

Am I contrite for
being ecstatic? Sorry
for joy? Life's elastic.

I love my yoga and
it's good for writing but no
pages get done there.

Did the numbers. Wow.
Is that really how much we
need just to get by?

"Happy Mother's Day,"
I tell Nana. "Wish I could
say the same to you."

Watched home shows like porn:
someday I'll get up, do it
myself. And I have.

I'm a spiral girl
living in a linear
world. Sometimes passing.

Type A Free Spirit.
Working hard to let the wind
blow me where it will.

Want is the new have.
Tops are the new bottoms.
New is the new new.

ACKNOWLEDGEMENTS

For years I was unable to do my "gratitude list" and I felt so ashamed! Unworthy. "Begin your day with a gratitude list," all the gurus say. OK. "Wake up being grateful." Right.

I tried. But I'd always start with the big stuff. Being alive, Greg, that I don't live in a totally fascistic state. Which lead me directly to thinking that I was going to die, that Greg was, that we did live in a totally fascistic state and I just wasn't brave enough to admit it. And while it's possible that these are also things to be grateful for, I was too busy freaking out to consider that. And I'm that pretty sure that feeling of panic, was not what the gurus had in mind when they advised gratitude.

Then I got fired, 9/11, one of my best friends died, the boyfriend of one of my other best friends died, my back went out and I was broke. One restless, Ambien-less night it occurred to me that since I was up I could do my morning gratitude list now. And since I was used to doing alphabetical games to try to fall asleep, I started with A. Not the biggest things first. Just something beginning with A. Maybe the Artichoke I'd had for lunch. It was fun, it was easy. I was grateful. I was sleeping before I got to M. And it's become a habit. A habit I am grateful for.

And for this book I give thanks to:

Greg Miller, first, last, and always.

Alignment—Anusara Yoga, Anthony and Rebecca Benenati and the City Yoga kula, JP, George Mariella

Beds and Breakfasts and Big-heartedness—Tracy Poust, Cindy Chupak, Larry and Emily Karaszewski, John Riggi and David Wendelman, Barbara Bestor, Rob Ramsey and Carol Schwartz, Joy Dickson, Pete and Cindy Caponera, Scott King, Sue Wolf,

Glenn Scantlebury and Lucy Phillips, Deirdre and Antonio Mendoza, The Kaizer/Moss Institute for Higher Learning, Jeanne O'Connor, Laura Kightlinger

Committment—The hard working staff at Soft Skull

Dreams—Baby

Enthusiasm—Merrill Markoe, Terry Sweeney and Lanier Laney, Scott Carter, Stephen Glass, Chris Young and John Kinnally, Terry Enroth, Greg Behrendt, Terry Danuser, Moon Zappa, Corny Koehl, Christina Radu, Chickie, Jaime Daley, Gary Janetti and Brad Goresky, Douglas Ross, Gail Chamberlain, Kiara Bailey

First readers—Jessica Bendinger, Jerry Stahl, Brad Kessler, Kate Robin, Daniel Kaizer

Gertrude Stein—Jane Cohen

Hook ups—Bruce Eric Kaplan, Bruce Tracy, Doug Budin, David Keeps, Adam Moss

Insights—Michael Patrick King, Bob Riley

Jewishness—Kitty and Hymie Chepovsky, Evan and Pam Kaizer, Rabbi Cooper

Kapotasana—Grace

Loving—Rita and Martin Lapides, Anita Cooper, Lambee

Magic—Dona McAdams

Naming—John C. Reilly and Alison Dickey, Carol Mann

Phone-a-friends—Julie Talen, Nicole Arbusto

Quiet—Palm Springs and those who helped get us here, Mae Cooper, Pete Buonocare, Robert Ramblas, Maxinne Lapiduss and Hilary Carlip, Andy Dick, Korakia, The Doves

Reliability—Alex Hinton and Andy Wombwell, Jaime Love

Showing up—Un-Cabaret audiences and performers, my students

Traveling—Michael and Karen and Isaac and Nathan Lapides, Susan Lichtman and Dennis Congdon

Un-Cabaret rooms—Jean Pierre Boccaro and Luna Park, Joe

Reynolds and M-Bar, Gary S. Mann and John Martin and the HBO Workspace, Jordan Peimer and the Skirball Cultural Center

Vibrational adjustment—Robot, JP, Virginia Shiraz, Sonia Choquette, Jenifer, Betty, The Integratron,

Wake up calls—Mr. Lee, Dr. Emoto, Doreen Virtue, David Icke, Angel, Greg Braeden, Living Oneness, Judy Toll

X-Factor—that which can't be named and must be thanked

Yes—Richard Nash, Elisabeth Weed, Fiora/Ghetto Gloss, James Joyce

Zzz's – Now and Zen, Teddy, The Ultimate Bed

photo credit: Lesley Bohm

Beth Lapides is a seeker, speaker and entertainer. She has appeared on many TV shows including *Politically Incorrect*, *The Today Show* and *Sex and the City*. She also hosted her own Un-Cabaret special on Comedy Central and a daily talk show on Comedy World Radio. She's a commentator for NPR's *All Things Considered*, an NEA winner and a former candidate for First Lady. She's written for the *Los Angeles Times*, *LA Weekly*, *The Realist*, and The Huffington Post. For more info about Beth's up-coming appearances, media projects and writing workshops: bethlapides.com.